Sport and My Body

Swimming

Charlotte Guillain

www.raintreepublishers.co.uk
Visit our website to find out more information about Raintree books.

To order:
☎ Phone +44 (0) 1865 888066
▤ Fax +44 (0) 1865 314091
▨ Visit www.raintreepublishers.co.uk

Raintree is an imprint of Capstone Global Library Limited, a company incorporated in England and Wales having its registered office at 7 Pilgrim Street, London, EC4V 6LB – Registered company number: 6695582

"Raintree" is a registered trademark of Pearson Education Limited, under licence to Capstone Global Library Limited

Edited by Siân Smith, Rebecca Rissman, and
  Charlotte Guillain
Designed by Joanna Hinton-Malivoire
Picture research by Ruth Blair
Production by Duncan Gilbert
Originated by Chroma Graphics (Overseas) Pte. Ltd
Printed and bound in China by South China Printing Company Ltd

ISBN 978 1 406 21113 9
13 12 11 10 09
10 9 8 7 6 5 4 3 2 1

British Library Cataloguing in Publication Data
Guillain, Charlotte.
  Swimming. -- (Sport and my body)
  1. Swimming--Physiological aspects--Juvenile literature.
  2. Swimming--Social aspects--Juvenile literature.
  I. Title II. Series
  613.7'16-dc22

Acknowledgements
We would like to thank the following for permission to reproduce photographs: Alamy pp.**10** (© Martin Strmiska), **19**, **23** (© Richard Levine); Corbis pp.**4** (Reix – Liewig/For Picture), **6** (Jan Butchofsky-Houser), **15** (Scott McDermott), **23** (Annie Griffiths Belt), **23** (Scott McDermott), **23** (Reix – Liewig/For Picture); Gett Images pp.**11** (Leander Baerenz/Photonica), **13** (David Madison), **16** (Tracy Frankel), **20** (ColorBlind Images); iStockphoto **22**, **22** (© Martin Pernter), **22** (© Rafa Irusta); Photolibrary pp.**8** (Purestock), **14** (Flirt Collection), **17**, **18** (Radius Images), **21** (Burke/Triolo Productions); Science Photo Library pp.**7**, **23** (Bill Bachmann); Shutterstock pp.**5** (© Gert Johannes Jacobus Vrey), **9** (© Sander Rom).

Cover photograph of swimmer reproduced with permission of Getty Images/China Photos. Back cover photographs reproduced with permission of iStockphoto: 1. child in swimming cap; 2. swimming goggles (© Martin Pernter).

Every effort has been made to contact copyright holders of material reproduced in this book. Any omissions will be rectified in subsequent printings if notice is given to the publishers.

Disclaimer
All the Internet addresses (URLs) given in this book were valid at the time of going to press. However, due to the dynamic nature of the Internet, some addresses may have changed, or sites may have changed or ceased to exist since publication. While the author and publisher regret any inconvenience this may cause readers, no responsibility for any such changes can be accepted by either the author or the publisher.

Contents

Some words are shown in bold, **like this**. You can find them in the glossary on page 23.

What is swimming?

Swimming is exercise we do in water.
You can swim in the sea or in a
swimming pool.

Some people swim in competitions and races. Other people just swim to keep fit and have fun.

How do I learn to swim?

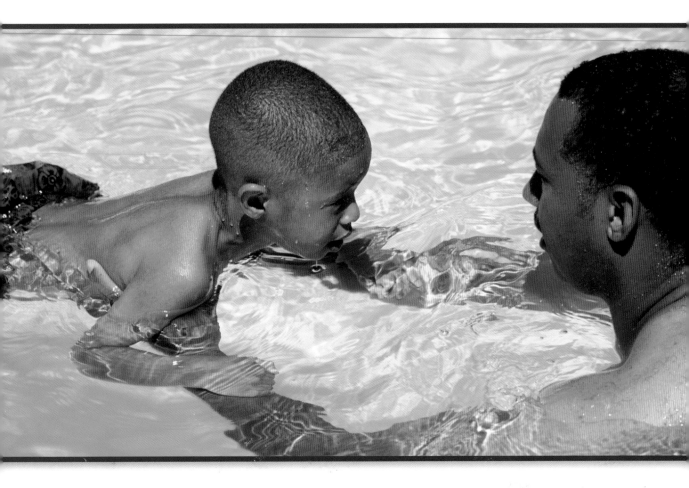

You need an adult to teach you how to swim. A teacher at your school or a swimming teacher could teach you at a swimming pool.

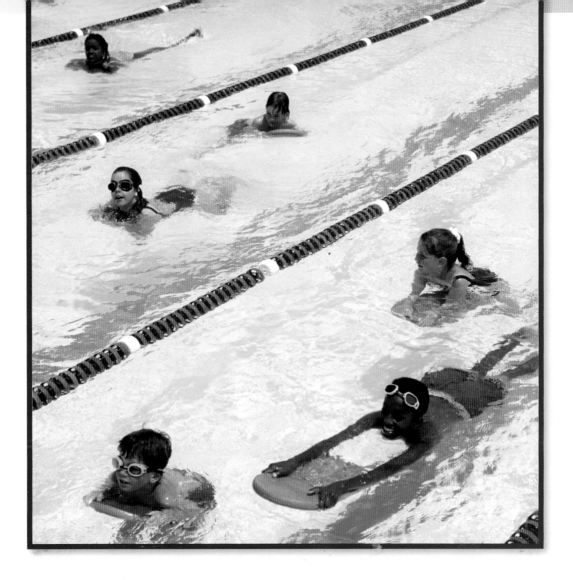

To start you need to get used to putting your face in the water. You might use **floats** to help you learn to swim.

How do I use my arms?

You use your arms to pull yourself through the water. You can move your arms in different ways, called **strokes**.

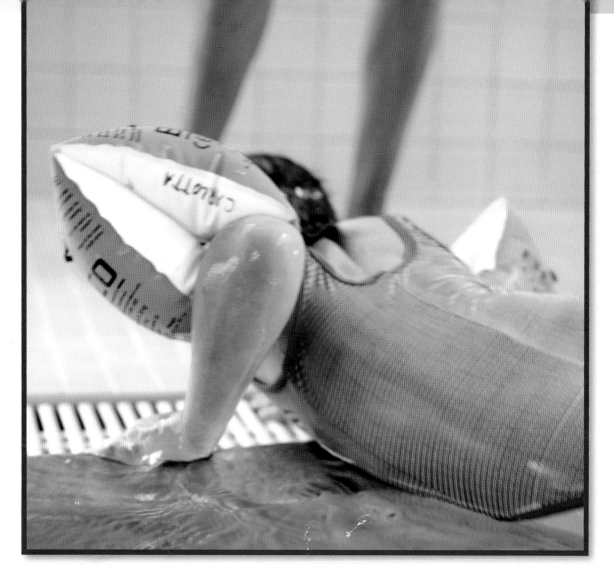

You can use your arms to push down on the side of the pool so you can climb out.

How do I use my legs?

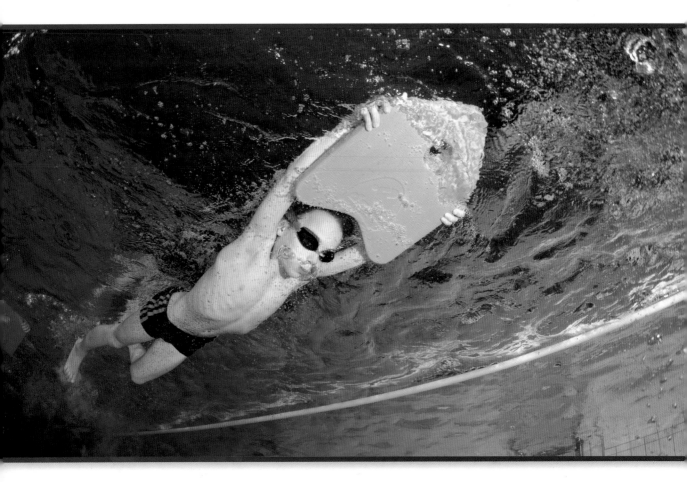

You use your legs to kick. This helps you to move through the water. When you kick hard, you swim faster.

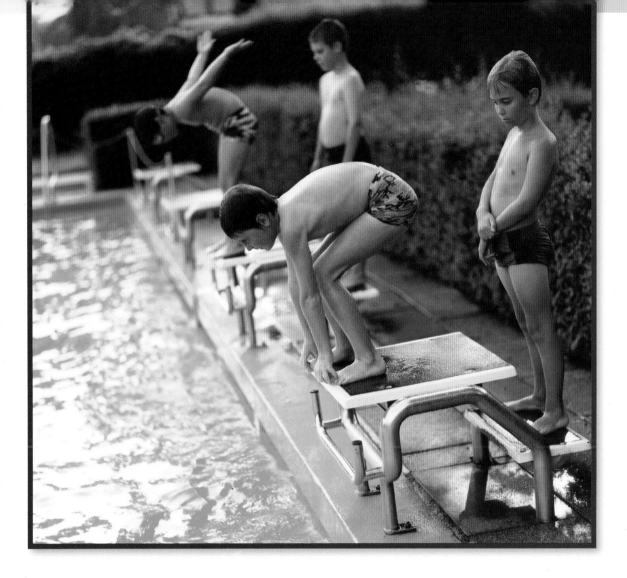

You use your legs when you jump or dive into the pool. You should bend your knees before you jump.

How do I use the rest of my body?

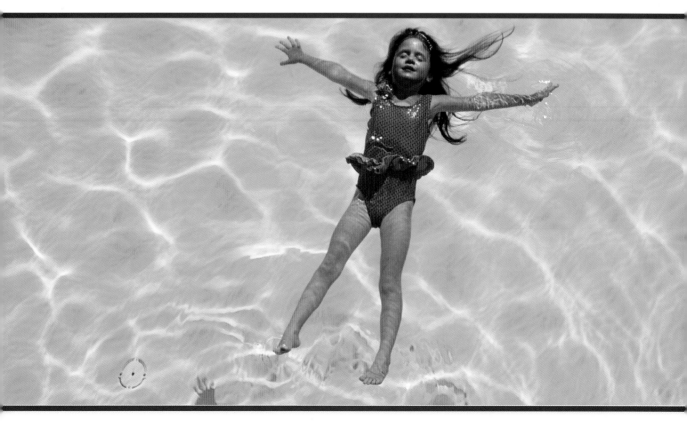

You can **float** on your back near the top of the water.

You learn how to hold your breath and open your eyes under water. You move your head up or to the side to breathe when you swim.

What happens to my body when I swim?

When you get into the pool the water might make you feel colder. As you swim you will feel warmer and you will breathe faster.

muscle

Your heart will start to beat faster.
The **muscles** in your arms and legs
will feel tired.

How does it feel to swim?

Swimming is a good way to have fun. You might make new friends as you swim together.

It feels good to get better at swimming. When you swim further or faster you might get a special badge or medal.

How do I stay safe swimming?

Always listen to your teacher or the **lifeguard**. Make sure you know the rules at the swimming pool.

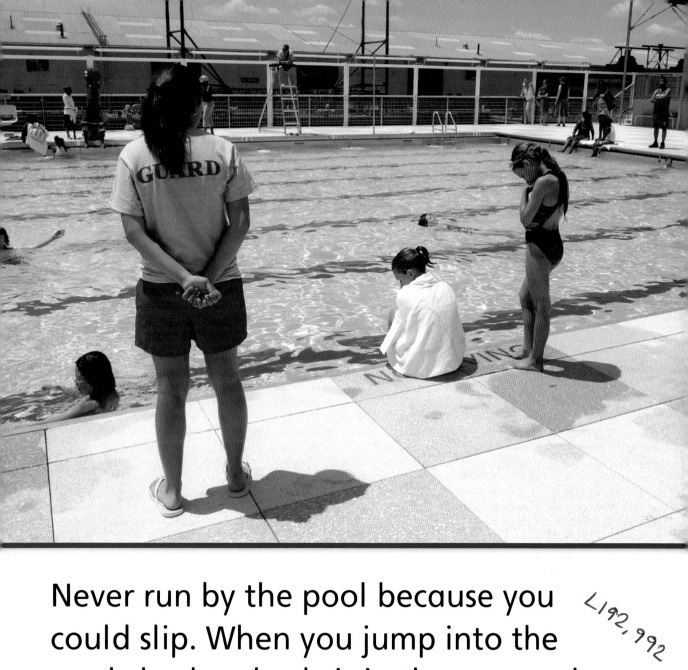

Never run by the pool because you could slip. When you jump into the pool check nobody is in the way and that the water is deep enough.

Does swimming make me healthy?

Swimming is good exercise and will help to keep you fit. To stay healthy you also need to get plenty of rest.

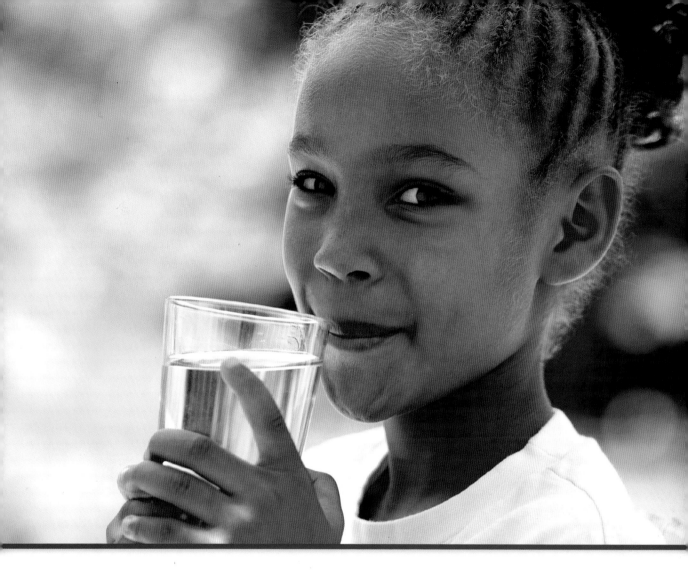

You should also eat healthy food every day and drink plenty of water.

Swimming equipment

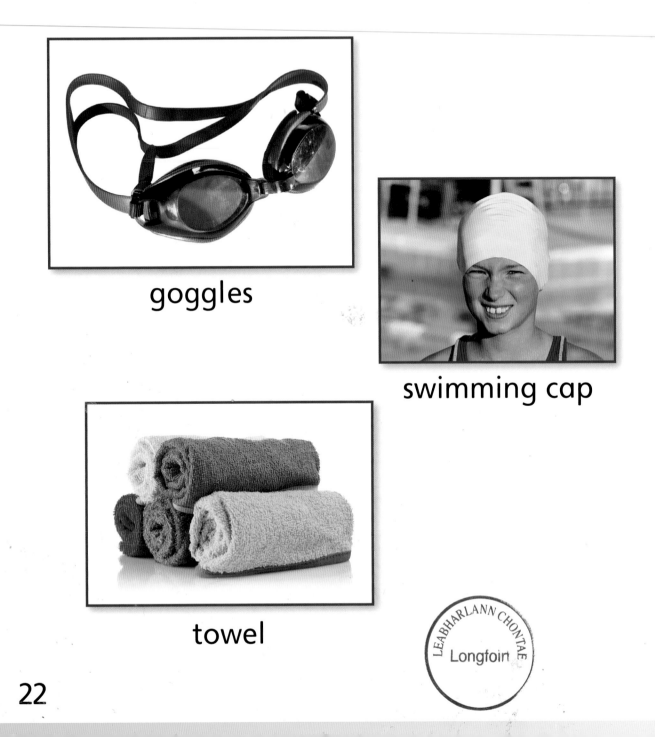

goggles

swimming cap

towel

Glossary

 float stay near the top of water

 floats things that float in water and can be used to help people learn to swim

 lifeguard someone who works at a swimming pool or on a beach, who helps people to stay safe in the water

 muscle part of your body that helps you to move. Exercise can make muscles bigger and stronger.

 stroke in swimming a stroke is a movement you make with your arms or legs to help you move through the water

Index

Find out more

http://kidshealth.org/kid/watch/out/water.html
Find out how to stay safe in and around water.

http://www.videojug.com/film/basic-swimming-strokes-for-young-children-5-7-years-2
This website includes some basic swimming strokes to help you practise.